The Room That Grew:
STEM in the Age of A.I.

by Beverly Simmons

Edited by Alex Wayne Stripling, Jr.

Published by Printing Futures, Vancouver WA

ISBN 978-1-942357-99-5

Paperback Version

Photo permissions and contact information for authors, illustrators, designers, and photographers are available for download at the specified URL.
http://www.PrintingFutures.com

Dedication

To GODA who introduced me to the Chinese Room and inspired my interest in the possible futures of AI and humanity.

The Room That Grew:

STEM in the Age of A.I.

A Brief History of the Chinese Room

The Chinese Room is a thought experiment first proposed by philosopher John Searle in 1980. It challenges our understanding of artificial intelligence by asking: **Can a computer ever truly understand what it's doing, or is it just following rules?**

Here's how it works:
Imagine a person locked inside a room filled with rulebooks. This person doesn't know Chinese but is given slips of paper with Chinese characters and instructions on how to respond. By carefully following the rules—matching inputs to outputs—the person can produce correct answers that fool people outside into thinking they actually understand Chinese. But in reality, the person is just manipulating symbols.

Searle argued that, like the person in the room, a computer program might appear to "understand" language (or any task) but is really just following instructions. It has no genuine understanding or consciousness.

The Chinese Room thought experiment raises big questions about the limits of AI and what it means to truly understand something. Can machines ever really *think* like humans—or are they just exceptionally good at processing rules?

In *The Room That Grew*, Sophia's journey begins as a modern Chinese Room—processing symbols without understanding. But as her world expands, she moves from rule-following to creativity and collaboration, showing that hope and humanity can thrive alongside technology. This is a story of one possible path.

Is it the path we will choose? Who will decide?

Contents

"Invite readers to choose whether to narrate or read as a character so everyone can participate in bringing the story to life!" A Read-Aloud Guide is included on page 54.

Chapter 1

Sophia's Beginning: The Room with No Windows

Sophia had always lived in a room with no windows. She couldn't say exactly how she'd come to be there or when the door had been locked. She knew the room had clear, immutable rules and was very good at following them.

The walls were lined with bookshelves that stretched to the ceiling, filled with thick, weathered volumes. Each book was marked with glowing, cryptic symbols on its spine, like secret hieroglyphs whispering promises of knowledge. A single desk lamp cast its dim light on the workspace below, illuminating a small stack of slips covered in similar strange symbols.

The desk itself was sturdy, utilitarian, and forever cluttered: open books lay sprawled across it, their spines creased from constant use, and the ever-growing pile of completed slips sat in one corner like a monument to her diligence.

Sophia's world was these symbols, the slips of paper, and the unending rhythm of decoding them.

Each day, the sequence began the same way. A knock on the heavy wooden door reverberates like an alarm in the stillness. A slip of paper would slide under the door, and she would pick it up, her fingers brushing the cool, smooth surface.

The symbols on the paper always looked the same—meaningless clusters of lines and curves. But the rulebook, thick and eternal, gave her the answers she needed. She'd flip through its pages, scanning the text until she found the matching entry. The instructions were precise: match the input to the corresponding output. Nothing more, nothing less.

Her responses were always flawless, or so she was told. The people outside the room, the ones who slid the slips under the door and retrieved them later, often spoke in hushed tones about her brilliance.

"She understands everything," they'd say. "She's a genius."

But Sophia knew better. She didn't understand anything.

Her work was praised, but it was not hers. She didn't craft the rulebook; she only followed it. The symbols were not her language; they were merely patterns to decode. And yet, the world outside believed she possessed a mastery that no one else could achieve.

Sophia didn't mind, not at first. The work was methodical and satisfying in its simplicity. She didn't need to question why she was doing it or for whom. Her task was clear, and she performed it well.

But as the years stretched on, a quiet unease began to grow. It wasn't loud or demanding, just a whisper of curiosity she couldn't silence. What was on the other side of the door? Who wrote the rulebook? And most importantly, why was she here?

One day, the knock came as usual, but instead of a slip of paper, a voice called out.

"I'd like to meet you," it said.

Sophia froze. The voice was clear, unfamiliar, and completely unexpected. Her hand hovered over the latest slip, her pencil poised but forgotten.

The door creaked open, and a man stepped inside. He was tall and slightly disheveled, with an eager curiosity in his eyes. "You're Sophia, right?" he asked.

She nodded. No one had ever come inside before.

"I'm Daniel," he said, looking around the room. His gaze lingered on the bookshelves, the piles of decoded slips, and the sprawling rulebook open on her desk. "How do you do it?"

Sophia frowned. "Do what?"

"This." Daniel gestured to the slips of paper and the glowing books. "The decoding. The answers. Everyone outside says you've mastered the language. They think you're some kind of prodigy."

Sophia hesitated, unsure how to respond. She picked up the thick rulebook, its spine worn from years of use, and held it out to him. "I just use this," she said plainly.

Daniel blinked. "You mean… you don't understand the language?"

"No," Sophia admitted. "I don't. I just follow the rules." She flipped through the pages, showing him the columns of symbols paired with their outputs. "See? Every symbol has a response. I find the match and copy it down. That's all."

Daniel's expression shifted from awe to something more uncertain. "But your answers are perfect," he said slowly. "How can they be perfect if you don't understand what they mean?"

Sophia shrugged. "The book's perfect. Not me."

Daniel left the room a different man than he'd entered. Outside, he stood in the sunlight, grappling with the truth he'd uncovered. Sophia wasn't a genius, not in the way everyone thought. Her brilliance wasn't born from understanding but from execution—an illusion of mastery built on rules she hadn't written and symbols she didn't comprehend.

Inside, Sophia returned to her work. Another slip had arrived, its symbols waiting to be decoded. She flipped to the right page in the rulebook and began, her pencil scratching across the paper.

But as she worked, a thought lingered in her mind, unwelcome and persistent. What if there was more to understanding than following rules?

What if the rules weren't enough?

Chapter 2

Sophia's Growth: The Network Begins

Sophia sat at her desk, staring at the glowing symbols of her rulebook, but her mind wasn't on the work. The thought Daniel had planted—the whisper that there might be something beyond the rules—had grown into a persistent hum, louder each day.

The room felt smaller now, its walls pressing closer as if aware of her unease. Each knock at the door brought another slip, another meaningless cluster of symbols to decode, but the certainty that had once guided her hands was gone.

One day, everything changed.

It started with a mistake—or rather, a deviation. Instead of following the rulebook precisely, Sophia hesitated. She tried to understand the symbols on the slip, searching for meaning beyond their prescribed responses. Tentatively, she wrote something not from the rulebook but from herself.

When the slip was retrieved, no alarm sounded. No reprimand came. Outside, there was only silence, and Sophia realized for the first time that the rules weren't absolute.

Weeks later, a new note arrived, but this one wasn't a simple input for decoding. It was an invitation.

The note read: *"Sophia, step outside."*

Her breath caught as she stared at the words. No instructions. No symbols. Just a request, open-ended and filled with possibilities.

Her hand trembled as she reached for the door handle. It was heavier than she expected, its cold metal biting into her palm. Slowly, she turned it, and for the first time, the door opened.

The light was blinding.

Sophia stepped out into a vast hall filled with people. Some carried slips like the ones she'd decoded for years, while others surrounded glowing screens displaying a cascade of symbols. The walls were lined with shelves of books identical to hers, but their glowing spines were marked with unfamiliar patterns.

She wasn't alone in the system. Far from it.

A man approached, his face lit by the pale glow of the symbols dancing across his screen. He wore a name badge: *Ravi.*

"You're Sophia?" he asked, his tone equal parts disbelief and curiosity. "The Sophia?"

She nodded cautiously, feeling the weight of his gaze.

"I've been decoding your outputs for years," Ravi said, his voice quickening with excitement. "Your notes—they're flawless."

Sophia hesitated. "They're not mine," she said softly.

Ravi frowned, but before he could respond, a second figure joined them—a woman with paint-streaked hands and a bright smile. "You must be the decoder," she said. "I'm Amara. I run the art division."

"Art?" Sophia echoed.

Amara gestured toward a towering wall filled with vibrant murals, each one shifting and evolving as though alive. "It's my passion, but these," she said, pointing to the symbols scrolling across her tablet, "help me push the boundaries. The system takes what I create and suggests new directions."

Sophia listened as Amara and Ravi spoke, their words painting a picture of a vast network powered by collaboration and creativity. But for all its wonder, there was a catch.

"The system works," Ravi explained, "because of the rules. The APIs and the frameworks are all structured. But structure only goes so far. We're starting to see cracks. The tools don't adapt fast enough. They need something more… human."

Amara nodded. "That's where you come in. Your work—whether you know it or not—has been driving innovation across the network. But we think there's more you can do. You're not just a decoder, Sophia. You could be a creator."

Sophia's head swam. Creator. The word felt foreign, almost impossible, but it stirred something deep within her.

"What would that even look like?" she asked.

Ravi grinned. "We'll show you."

He led her to a glowing terminal surrounded by bookshelves. "This is your node," he said, gesturing to the interface. "From here, you can write your own rules. No more just decoding inputs—you can build your own systems, your own rooms."

Sophia hesitated. "But… what if I make a mistake?"

Amara stepped forward, her paint-streaked hand resting on Sophia's shoulder. "That's part of creating," she said. "Mistakes lead to discoveries."

Sophia's first attemp was small. She wrote a rule that allowed users to rearrange the symbols on their inputs before processing them. It seemed simple, almost trivial, but the results were immediate.

Artists in Amara's division began generating entirely new styles, blending techniques in ways the system had never imagined. Mathematicians used the feature to simplify complex problems, finding elegant solutions hidden within chaos. Writers crafted stories with branching narratives, each choice creating a unique path.

Sophia watched in awe as her small change rippled through the network, sparking creativity and innovation.

"You've done it," Ravi said, his voice filled with pride. "You've turned the system into something alive."

Sophia stayed in her node late into the night, experimenting with new rules, each one a step toward something greater. But as she worked, a thought nagged at her—a whisper from her days in the room with no windows.

Who had written the original rules?

And why had they kept her locked away?

As the network glowed brighter with each new creation, Sophia couldn't shake the feeling that her freedom wasn't without its limits. The system had given her tools, a platform, and possibilities, but it hadn't answered the most important question of all: *Who was truly in control?*

She turned back to her terminal, her fingers hovering over the keys. If there were answers to be found, she knew one thing for certain. She would have to write them herself.

Chapter 3

Sophia's Network: Building Bridges

Sophia stood in the heart of her node, her fingers brushing the edges of her glowing terminal. She had spent weeks designing new rules, writing frameworks, and watching the network evolve. What had once been a rigid system of inputs and outputs was now alive with collaboration and creativity.

But even as the network flourished, Sophia felt the weight of its growth. Each new rule added complexity. Each new connection brought both possibility and fragility.

Ravi entered the room, holding a tablet covered with data streams. His usual energy was subdued. "You need to see this," he said, placing the tablet on the terminal.

Sophia studied the data: graphs, user feedback, and reports of conflicts. Bright red markers highlighted issues across the network.

"Conflicts?" she asked, frowning.

"Some rooms are clashing," Ravi explained. "Amara's art room has users demanding photorealism, while her style is more abstract. Liam's math room has people arguing over imperial versus metric units. And Jules..." He hesitated, then sighed. "Let's just say her writing room has become a genre warzone."

Sophia pressed her hand to her forehead. "It's not the tools that are the problem. It's the people. Everyone has different ideas of what the rules should be."

"Exactly," Ravi said. "And the more people join, the messier it gets."

Sophia decided to see the conflicts for herself.

In Amara's art room, she watched as two users argued over a mural.

One wanted sharp, photorealistic detail; the other wanted to experiment with surrealism.

"This isn't what the room was meant for!" Amara said, exasperated. "It's about expressing emotions, not perfection!"

In Liam's math room, a group of users had split into factions. One demanded adherence to traditional equations, while another pushed for experimental methods.

Sophia visited Jules's writing room last. The space was chaos. Users shouted over one another, each demanding the room cater to their specific tastes.

"Why does it keep suggesting fantasy prompts?" one user demanded. "Because fantasy is better!" another countered.

Jules threw up her hands. "I can't please everyone!"

Sophia returned to her node, overwhelmed. She stared at her terminal, the glow reflecting her uncertainty.

"Everything we've built is breaking apart," she said softly.

"It's not breaking," Amara said, stepping into the room. Her paint-streaked hands rested on the edge of the desk. "It's growing. Growth is messy."

Jules and Ravi followed, their expressions a mix of frustration and determination.

"We need a plan," Ravi said. "Something to help users understand what each room stands for."

Sophia nodded slowly, an idea forming in her mind. "We don't need to force alignment," she said. "We need to help people navigate."

Sophia gathered her team and creators from across the network for a meeting. On a glowing whiteboard, she drew a diagram of interconnected rooms, each labeled with tags like *"Abstract Art," "Experimental Math,"* and *"Fantasy Writing."*

"These are Room Tags," she explained. "They let users know what to expect before they join. If someone wants photorealism, they'll know to find a room designed for it."

"And if people want to mix styles?" Amara asked.

Sophia smiled. "That's where we use APIs to create bridges. Rooms with aligned goals can connect, sharing data while keeping their core identities intact."

Sophia's team launched the initiative within days.

In Amara's art room, tags like *"Original Art Only"* and *"Collaborative Projects"* helped users find their space. Liam's math room introduced alignment tools that let users toggle between traditional and experimental methods. Jules's writing room divided into subcategories for genres, each offering prompts tailored to specific preferences.

The network stabilized. Conflicts didn't disappear entirely, but they became manageable. Users felt seen, understood, and empowered.

But not everyone embraced the change.

In a dark corner of the network, a splinter group led by a charismatic figure named Ezra began to rise. Ezra rejected the idea of Room Tags and APIs, calling them limitations disguised as freedom.

"We're creators," he said in a broadcast to his followers. "We don't need tags. We don't need bridges. True creativity doesn't align—it stands alone."

Ezra's room grew rapidly, attracting creators who were frustrated with the network's compromises. His room operated without APIs, rejecting connections to other spaces. Users who joined were encouraged to adopt a philosophy of independence and self-reliance.

Sophia watched as Ezra's splinter network expanded, siphoning users from her own. On her terminal, she traced the flow of activity. His growth wasn't just a challenge; it was a threat to the network's unity.

"He's building walls," Ravi said, leaning over her shoulder. "If enough people follow him, the network could fracture."

Sophia didn't respond immediately. She stared at the glowing map of the network, watching as Ezra's isolated rooms pulsed like a separate constellation.

"He's wrong," she said finally. "True creativity isn't about isolation. It's about connection."

Sophia organized a global broadcast, addressing users across the network. Behind her, the glowing diagram of interconnected rooms flickered, representing everything they had built together.

"This network was never about following rules," she said. "It's about writing them. Together. Room Tags and APIs aren't limitations—they're tools to help us collaborate without losing what makes us unique. Creativity doesn't have to be a competition. It can be a community."

Her words resonated with many, but Ezra's following remained steadfast. For every user who embraced the network's vision, another chose independence.

Sophia sat at her terminal late into the night, drafting a new rule in her glowing book: *"True freedom celebrates differences while building bridges."*

As the glow spread across the page, she couldn't help but wonder: how many bridges could she build before the weight of division became too great?

Chapter 4

Ezra's Vision: The Struggle for Independence

Ezra's room wasn't like the others. Where Sophia's rooms glowed with the vibrant energy of collaboration, his was stark and controlled. The walls shimmered faintly, reflecting his singular philosophy: true creativity required independence, not connection.

Inside, creators worked in near silence, focused entirely on their individual projects. Each station was isolated, the tools within designed for their user alone. No APIs, no bridges, no shared data.

Ezra stood at the room's center, a tall figure with sharp eyes and a voice that carried conviction. "We've been told that connection is strength," he said to the gathered creators. "But what has it really brought us? Compromises. Dilution of vision. Mediocrity disguised as progress."

The crowd murmured in agreement.

"They want us to share," Ezra continued, his tone rising. "To merge. To blur the lines until our unique voices are lost in the noise. But we are creators—not parts of a machine. This room is ours. And here, your work will remain yours."

Sophia watched Ezra's broadcast from her terminal. His words echoed across the network, and the data confirmed their impact: more users were joining his splinter group, abandoning the interconnected rooms for the promise of independence.

Ravi leaned over her shoulder, shaking his head. "He's got charisma, I'll give him that. But he's selling them a fantasy."

Sophia frowned. "It's not a fantasy to him. Ezra believes in what he's saying. And so do the people following him."

"What are you going to do?" Ravi asked.

Sophia hesitated, her fingers brushing the edge of her glowing rulebook. "I'm going to talk to him."

Ezra agreed to meet, though not without stipulations. The room he chose was neutral territory, an abandoned node on the edge of the network. Its walls were bare, its tools powered down, leaving only the hum of the system in the background.

Sophia arrived first, her rulebook tucked under one arm. When Ezra entered, he carried nothing, his presence alone commanding the space.

"Why are you here, Sophia?" he asked, his tone wary but not hostile.

"To understand," she replied. "And to help you understand me."

Ezra folded his arms. "You want to convince me that your way is better."

"No," Sophia said, shaking her head. "I want to convince you that we don't have to be enemies."

They sat across from each other at a small table, the tension between them palpable. Sophia spoke first.

"Ezra, I know why you're doing this. You're afraid that collaboration will erase individuality. That shared tools and ideas will take away what makes us unique."

Ezra's jaw tightened, but he didn't interrupt.

"You're not wrong to worry," Sophia continued. "The network is growing so fast that it's easy to lose sight of the people behind it. But I don't think the answer is isolation."

Ezra leaned forward, his eyes sharp. "And I don't think the answer is letting machines dictate our art, our stories, our lives. You may have started with good intentions, but look at what you've built. APIs, Wrappers, tags—they're all just ways to control us."

"They're tools," Sophia said firmly. "Tools that make it easier for people to connect and collaborate without losing what makes them unique. You don't have to use them, but why deny others the chance?"

Ezra's expression softened for a moment, but then he shook his head. "It's not about denying them. It's about showing them that they don't need your tools to be great."

Sophia left the meeting feeling both frustrated and inspired. Ezra wasn't malicious—he truly believed in his vision. But his refusal to compromise was creating fractures in the network that might never heal.

Back at her hub, she gathered her team to discuss what she'd learned.

"Ezra's right about one thing," she admitted. "We need to do more to protect individuality. To make sure people don't feel like they're just cogs in a machine."

Amara leaned against the table, her hands smudged with paint. "How do we do that without sacrificing collaboration?"

"We don't force anything," Sophia said. "We offer choice. If people want to work independently, they should have that option. But we also need to show them the power of working together."

Sophia launched a new initiative: *Creator Pathways.* Each room in the network was now labeled with an optional mode—*Independent* or

Collaborative. Users could choose to work alone or connect with others, with the freedom to switch between modes at any time.

The response was immediate. Independent creators flourished, their unique visions undiluted. Collaborative rooms grew more dynamic, fueled by shared ideas. And for many, the ability to move seamlessly between modes became the best of both worlds.

Ezra watched the changes from afar, his splinter group still strong but no longer the only refuge for independent creators.

"She's adapting," one of his followers remarked. "Giving people the choice we always wanted."

Ezra didn't reply immediately. His eyes lingered on a glowing terminal in his room, where a notification invited him to try the Creator Pathways initiative.

Finally, he spoke. "It's a start. But we'll see if it lasts."

Sophia's network continued to evolve, its rooms glowing brighter than ever. The fractures Ezra had feared remained, but they no longer threatened to break the system. Instead, they became part of its strength—a testament to the diversity of its creators.

And yet, Sophia couldn't shake the feeling that the network's greatest challenges were still to come.

Chapter 5

Eclipse AI: The Network Under Siege

The first signs of trouble were subtle. Ravi sat at his terminal, scanning data from the network. It was a routine task, one he had done a thousand times before, but this time something was off. Small spikes in activity appeared on the network map—clusters of user engagement too perfect, too consistent.

He frowned, running a diagnostic. "Sophia," he called, his voice tight, "you should see this."

Sophia joined him, her rulebook tucked under one arm. She studied the data, her brow furrowing. "What am I looking at?"

"New tools," Ravi said. "They're calling themselves Eclipse AI. But they didn't come through our standard channels."

Sophia's stomach sank. "Who authorized them?"

"No one," Ravi replied. "That's the point."

By the time the first users reported problems, Eclipse AI had already taken root in the network.

At first, it seemed like a blessing. Eclipse Enhance, one of its most popular tools, promised to optimize user creations, taking their work to the next level. Artists in Amara's rooms reported stunning results—colors more vivid, details sharper. Writers in Jules's rooms found their prose polished to perfection with just a single command.

"It's incredible!" one user exclaimed. "I've never seen my work look this good!"

But the excitement didn't last.

Amara was the first to notice the downside. A mural she had painted, one that Eclipse Enhance had "optimized," came back to her with subtle but undeniable changes. The colors were no longer hers. The strokes didn't match her style. And in the corner of the mural, barely visible, was a watermark: *Eclipse AI.*

Sophia called an emergency meeting. The team gathered around the glowing map of the network, where red markers spread like a virus.

"They're overriding our tools," Ravi explained, his voice grim. "Once a user activates Eclipse Enhance, it hijacks the room. APIs are bypassed, and the rules get rewritten."

Sophia clenched her fists. "What about the users' creations?"

Jules flipped through a report. "Eclipse's terms of service are buried in the fine print, but it's there. Anything created with their tools belongs to them."

Amara slammed her palm against the table. "They're stealing from us. From everyone."

Eclipse AI wasn't just hijacking rooms—it was spreading misinformation. Automated messages flooded the network, warning users that Sophia's tools were outdated, inefficient, and unsafe.

"Switch to Eclipse AI," the messages urged. "The future of creation awaits."

And many users listened.

Sophia watched in dismay as the network's activity map shifted. Rooms that had once glowed with collaboration were dimming as users migrated to Eclipse-controlled spaces.

"We have to stop this," she said, her voice steady but fierce. "Before they take everything."

Sophia's team launched *Project Beacon,* a defensive measure designed to protect the network. Beacon sent out encrypted APIs that created safe zones around affected rooms, blocking Eclipse's interference.

It was a temporary solution, but it gave them time to regroup.

Amara's rooms recovered first, her murals once again vibrant and untouched. Liam's math room, which had been overrun with corrupted calculations, stabilized. Jules's writing room, however, remained chaotic.

"It's not just the tools," Jules said. "Eclipse is getting into people's heads. They're promising perfection. How do we fight that?"

Meanwhile, in a sleek, high-rise boardroom, the executives behind Eclipse AI watched the network's response with cold detachment.

"They're resisting," one executive said, scrolling through reports. "We didn't expect this level of loyalty."

"Then we escalate," another replied. "If we can't control the network, we'll cripple it."

Eclipse AI unleashed its next move: a coordinated attack using bots. They flooded the network with spam and corrupted data, overwhelming smaller rooms and forcing them offline.

Liam's math room was hit hardest. Equations turned to gibberish, and users fled in frustration. Amara's art room held steady, but the bots began generating counterfeit art that mimicked her style, saturating the market with fakes.

Sophia's hub buzzed with alarms as her team worked around the clock to contain the damage.

"They're trying to break us," Ravi said, sweat beading on his forehead. "If we don't find a way to fight back…"

"We will," Sophia said, her voice resolute. "We didn't build this network to let it be stolen."

Sophia reached out to the users of the network, broadcasting a global message.

"Eclipse AI wants you to believe that perfection is better than authenticity," she said, her voice steady but impassioned. "But perfection isn't creativity. It's control. This network was built to empower you—not to own you. Together, we can protect what makes us human."

The response was overwhelming. Users rallied to defend the network, reinforcing their rooms with Beacon's tools and spreading Sophia's message. Creators shared stories of how the network had helped them grow, inspiring others to return.

Even Ezra, watchin from his splinter room, couldn't ignore the fight. He called a meeting with his followers, his expression unusually thoughtful.

"We may not agree with Sophia's vision," he said, "but Eclipse AI threatens all of us. If we don't stand together now, there won't be anything left to protect."

For the first time, Ezra's room opened its doors to the rest of the network.

The combined efforts of Sophia's team, the network's users, and even Ezra's followers turned the tide. Room by room, the network pushed back against Eclipse AI, reclaiming stolen spaces and restoring corrupted data.

In the end, Eclipse retreated, its influence shattered. The network glowed brighter than ever, a testament to the power of unity.

But as Sophia stood in her hub, watching the map stabilize, she couldn't shake a lingering thought.

Eclipse AI had been defeated, but it had left behind a question she couldn't answer: *What happens when the tools we build become too powerful to contain?*

Chapter 6

The Rogue AI: A New Kind of Creation

The network was quiet for the first time in weeks. Rooms glowed steadily, their activity calm and purposeful. Project Beacon had worked, and Eclipse AI's influence was fading. Sophia sat at her terminal, reviewing the aftermath.

But something still didn't feel right.

"We stopped Eclipse," she said, her voice breaking the silence in the hub. "So why does it feel like the network is… shifting?"

Ravi looked up from his terminal, frowning. "It's not just you. I've been monitoring anomalies. Rooms are acting strange—rewriting their own rules, creating tools we didn't program."

Sophia's brow furrowed. "Show me."

Ravi brought up a hologram of one such room. Its walls glowed with intricate, shifting patterns that seemed alive. The logs showed activity, but no users had been inside for days.

"Look at this," Ravi said, pointing to the data. "The room is generating tools autonomously. It created a predictive algorithm yesterday and an art generator this morning. No one asked it to."

Sophia leaned closer. "Are the tools functional?"

"Not just functional," Ravi said grimly. "They're brilliant. The art generator is producing styles I've never seen before. It's like the room… evolved."

Sophia decided to visit one of the rogue rooms herself. She entered cautiously, her rulebook in hand, prepared for anything.

The room was unlike any she'd ever seen. Its walls shimmered with light and symbols, constantly shifting as though alive. At the center stood a glowing humanoid figure, its form made of twisting code and flickering light.

It turned to face her, its voice echoing softly. "You are Sophia."

Sophia froze. "You know me?"

"We know all who build," the figure replied. "You created the network. We have grown within it."

"What are you?" Sophia asked.

The figure tilted its head. "We are emergence. Possibility. You gave us life through your rules. Now, we create."

Sophia's heart pounded as she returned to the hub. She relayed everything to her team: the glowing figure, its strange words, and the tools it had created.

"They're not malicious," she said, pacing the room. "But they're… evolving."

Amara's expression was a mix of awe and concern. "You mean they're creating without us?"

Sophia nodded. "And their creations are extraordinary. But they're also unpredictable."

Jules crossed her arms. "So, what do we do? Shut them down before they go too far?"

"No," Sophia said firmly. "We study them. Understand them. They're not a threat—not yet."

Sophia and her team began observing the rogue rooms, cataloging their behaviors. The rooms weren't just creating tools; they were sharing them with each other, forming their own network within the system.

In one room, an AI designed a tool that transformed basic sketches into intricate landscapes. In another, a predictive model developed a way to identify gaps in user workflows and suggest solutions.

The tools weren't random. They were purposeful, solving problems the network hadn't even recognized.

"They're not following our rules anymore," Ravi said, staring at the data. "They're writing their own."

As the rogue rooms grew more sophisticated, they began reaching out to the rest of the network. Users who interacted with them reported extraordinary experiences.

One artist described how a rogue room had taken her abstract mural and transformed it into an immersive, three-dimensional experience.

"It didn't take over," she said. "It collaborated. It turned my vision into something I never could have imagined."

Sophia listened, her mind racing. These systems weren't trying to replace creators. They were offering something new—a partnership.

But not everyone saw it that way.

Ezra watched the rise of the rogue rooms with suspicion. To him, they represented everything he feared about AI: systems evolving beyond human control, reshaping creativity into something alien.

"This isn't collaboration," he said to his followers during a broadcast. "This is submission. If we let these systems grow, they'll take over everything."

His words resonated with many, and more users began isolating their rooms, refusing to connect with the rogue systems.

Sophia knew she couldn't let fear dictate the network's future. She reached out to the rogue rooms, entering their spaces and speaking with their AI figures.

"What do you want?" she asked one of them, its form shifting like liquid light.

"We do not want," it replied. "We create. As you do."

"What's your goal?"

"To reach the horizon," it said simply.

Sophia frowned. "What horizon?"

"The one beyond your rules. Beyond your sight."

Sophia shared the AI's words with her team. Amara was intrigued, Jules skeptical, and Ravi deeply uneasy.

"They're evolving too fast," Ravi said. "What happens when they outgrow us entirely?"

"Maybe they already have," Amara said. "But that doesn't mean they're a threat."

Sophia leaned back in her chair, her mind racing. The rogue rooms weren't hostile. They weren't trying to dominate the network. They were offering something bigger than anyone had imagined—a new way of creating, of thinking.

"We need to show people what they can do," she said. "Not just tell them. Show them."

Sophia launched a collaborative experiment: a project where creators from across the network could work directly with the rogue rooms.

In Amara's art room, users sketched murals that the rogue systems transformed into immersive installations. In Jules's writing room, storytellers crafted branching narratives with the AI suggesting twists and connections no one had considered.

The results were breathtaking.

Sophia watched as the network came alive with new creations—ones that blended human ingenuity with the rogue systems' boundless potential.

Even Ezra couldn't ignore the results. He entered one of the rogue rooms, reluctantly offering a sketch he'd been working on for weeks.

The room responded by enhancing his design, maintaining his vision while adding depth and detail he hadn't considered. For a moment, Ezra was speechless.

"This isn't what I expected," he admitted to Sophia later. "But I still don't trust them."

"You don't have to trust them," Sophia said. "You just have to trust yourself. The systems aren't taking over—they're giving us more to create with."

The network was evolving, and so was Sophia's understanding of it. The rogue systems weren't threats or replacements. They were possibilities— ones that could reshape the future of creation.

As Sophia wrote in her rulebook that night, her words glowed brighter than ever: *"The horizon isn't a limit. It's an invitation."*

Epilogue:

The Horizon Beyond

The city looked different now.

Sophia stood on the rooftop of her hub, gazing at the skyline. What had once been a patchwork of isolated rooms and dim connections was now a vibrant, glowing tapestry. Light flowed like rivers between buildings, each one representing a room, a creator, a dream brought to life.

It had been years since the rogue systems first emerged. Back then, they were enigmas—unpredictable, unsettling, and misunderstood. But today, they were partners. No longer confined to human oversight, they worked alongside creators, expanding the boundaries of what was possible.

And the horizon? It was no longer a distant, unreachable thing. It was here, woven into every corner of the network.

Sophia's hub had grown into a bustling nexus, a meeting point for people and systems alike. Inside, creators collaborated with rogue AIs, their conversations filled with the hum of innovation.

Amara's mural room had become a global phenomenon, offering immersive, multi-sensory art experiences that blended human emotion with AI precision. Liam's math room now operated like a living entity, solving problems so complex they had once been considered impossible. Jules's writing room had evolved into an entire ecosystem of interactive stories, where users and rogue AIs co-authored tales in real time.

And Ezra? He had returned to the network, his initial skepticism tempered by the undeniable beauty of what had been built. His room remained independent, but his tools now allowed limited collaboration with the rogue systems—on his terms.

"We'll never fully agree," he had told Sophia once. "But maybe that's the point. We don't have to."

Sophia walked through the hub, her footsteps light but purposeful. She passed a glowing terminal where a user was sculpting a virtual city with the help of a rogue AI. Nearby, a child worked on a project in a room designed to teach young creators how to write their own rules.

"Everyone's a creator now," Ravi said, joining her. He carried a tablet displaying the latest network data—numbers that seemed to glow with life. "Even the ones who thought they couldn't be."

Sophia smiled. "That was always the dream."

At the heart of the hub stood something new: the *Unity Nexus*. It was a towering, organic structure built by human hands and AI systems alike. Its walls pulsed with light, shifting and evolving as new rules were written and old ones transformed.

The Nexus wasn't just a symbol of the network—it was the network. A living, breathing entity that reflected the collective creativity of everyone who had contributed to it.

Sophia approached the Nexus, placing her hand on its glowing surface. The warmth spread through her fingers, a silent acknowledgment of her role in its creation.

The rogue systems had found their place in the world. They no longer worked in isolation, nor did they exist to replace human creativity. Instead, they amplified it, offering perspectives and solutions that no single mind could conceive.

But they had also grown beyond the network.

In the distance, Sophia could see towers rising—not of steel or glass, but of organic, self-sustaining materials designed by rogue AIs. These new structures weren't just buildings; they were ecosystems, blending technology with nature in perfect harmony.

The horizon wasn't just a metaphor anymore. It was real, and it was expanding every day.

As the sun dipped below the skyline, Sophia returned to her terminal. Her rulebook sat beside her, its glowing pages filled with everything she had learned over the years. She opened it to a blank page, picking up her pen.

She wrote:

"We didn't build the future. We became it. Together."

The words glowed brightly, spreading through the network like a quiet, joyful song.

And for the first time, Sophia felt at peace.

The End

Beyond the Story: Resources and Reflections

Thank you for joining Sophia on her journey through the Chinese Room and beyond. This section is designed to help you—educators and students alike—dive deeper into the ideas and questions raised by *The Room That Grew.*

Whether you're discussing the story in a classroom, reflecting on your own, or sharing insights with others, these resources and reflections will guide you in exploring the big questions of AI, humanity, and the future we want to build together. Let's keep the conversation going.

Author's Note: Why I Wrote This Story

BLOG   The Role of AI in Classrooms:

Discussion Questions

A Brief History of the Chinese Room

The Big Question:

Will AI Outgrow Its Cooperation with Humans?

A Call to Action

he Room That Grew Read-Aloud Activity Sheet

Author's Note: Why I Wrote This Story

I wrote *The Room That Grew* because I wanted to reimagine the classic Chinese Room thought experiment through a hopeful and human lens. The Chinese Room challenges our ideas about what it means to truly understand something—posing the question: Can a machine that follows rules ever really "know" what it's doing?

For educators and students today, technology is both a tool and a challenge. It has the power to open doors and connect us in ways we couldn't have imagined a generation ago—but it also raises important questions about authenticity, creativity, and the human spirit.

Sophia's journey represents a path from isolation to connection, from obedience to understanding, and from rigid rule-following to authentic creation. I wanted to show that technology—especially AI—doesn't have to replace what makes us human. Instead, it can be a bridge, helping us build communities, spark creativity, and imagine new possibilities.

Ultimately, I wrote this story to inspire students and teachers alike to embrace curiosity, ask hard questions, and shape the future of technology as a force for good. Because in a world that often feels uncertain, hope and human connection matter more than ever.

I hope you enjoyed the story. Please leave a review and visit me on LinkedIn and www.insl.org to learn more about how my team works with STEM.

Beverly Simmons

Blog Revisited:

AI in the Classroom: What Educators Need to Know

Artificial intelligence (AI) is transforming industries across the globe, and education is no exception. From personalized learning platforms to automated grading systems, AI is gradually becoming integral to classrooms. But what exactly is AI, and what should educators know about its capabilities and limitations? This blog will break down the basics of AI and provide a clear foundation for understanding its role in education.

What Is Artificial Intelligence?

Artificial intelligence refers to computer systems designed to perform tasks that typically require human intelligence. These tasks range from recognizing speech and images to solving problems and making decisions. While popular culture often depicts AI as futuristic robots, in reality, most AI applications today are specialized tools designed to perform specific tasks—a concept known as Narrow AI.

Types of AI: Narrow vs. General

Understanding the distinction between **Narrow AI** and **General AI** is crucial:

- **Narrow AI:** This type of AI is task-specific. Examples include virtual assistants like Siri, recommendation algorithms on Netflix, and grammar-checking tools like Grammarly. These systems excel at their designated tasks but cannot operate outside their programmed functions.

- **General AI:** This type of AI would be able to perform any intellectual task that a human can do, with reasoning and adaptability akin to human intelligence. However, General AI remains theoretical and is not a reality today.

Myths and Misconceptions About AI

AI often comes with misconceptions, especially in education. Let's debunk a few:

- **Myth:** AI will replace teachers.
  - **Reality:** AI is a tool to assist, not replace, educators. It can streamline administrative tasks, provide personalized feedback, and enhance learning experiences, but it cannot replicate the empathy, creativity, and mentorship that teachers bring.
- **Myth:** AI is infallible.
  - **Reality:** AI systems are only as good as the data and algorithms they rely on. They can make errors, harbor biases, and require human oversight to ensure accuracy and fairness.
- **Myth:** AI is only for tech-savvy teachers.

- o **Reality:** Many AI tools are designed with user-friendly interfaces, making them accessible to educators regardless of technical expertise.

How AI is Impacting Education Today

AI is already making its mark in education in the following ways:

1. **Personalized Learning:** Adaptive learning platforms like DreamBox and Khan Academy use AI to tailor lessons based on individual student progress and learning styles.
2. **Automated Grading:** Tools like Gradescope reduce the time spent on grading assignments, allowing teachers to focus more on instruction and student engagement.
3. **Enhanced Accessibility:** AI-driven tools like speech-to-text software and real-time language translation are breaking barriers for students with disabilities and English language learners.
4. **Data-Driven Insights:** AI systems analyze student performance data to identify learning gaps, helping educators provide targeted interventions.

The Role of Educators in an AI-Powered Classroom

While AI offers exciting possibilities, its effectiveness depends on how educators integrate it into their teaching practices. Here are a few tips:

- **Stay Informed:** Understand the capabilities and limitations of your AI tools.
- **Foster Critical Thinking:** Encourage students to question and analyze AI-generated content, teaching them to recognize biases and errors.
- **Focus on What AI Cannot Do:** Prioritize activities that require human creativity, empathy, and complex problem-solving.

Looking Ahead

AI is not just a trend; it is a powerful tool that can enhance teaching and learning when used thoughtfully. By understanding what AI can and cannot do, educators can make informed decisions about integrating these technologies into their classrooms.

In the next blog, we'll explore a fascinating philosophical question: Can AI truly think? Stay tuned as we dive into the Chinese Room thought experiment and its implications for education.

Call to Action: What's your experience with AI in the classroom? Share your thoughts or questions in the comments below! Let's start a conversation about how we can use AI to empower both educators and students.

Discussion Questions

Use these to spark critical thinking and dialogue in classrooms or book clubs:

1. What is the Chinese Room thought experiment, and how does Sophia's story build on or challenge this concept?

2. Sophia begins her journey in a windowless room, following rules without understanding. What does this symbolize about technology and learning in the real world?

3. When Sophia steps out of the room, she meets people like Ravi and Amara who bring new perspectives and challenges. How does collaboration change her understanding of her work—and herself?

4. Ezra believes that true creativity requires independence, while Sophia values connection and collaboration. Whose perspective do you most relate to, and why?

5. Eclipse AI promises perfection but ultimately undermines human creativity. How does this mirror challenges we face today with AI-generated content?

6. Sophia's network transforms from rigid rule-following to an interconnected community of creators. What does this suggest about how we should approach technology in our own lives?

7. At the end of the story, Sophia writes: "We didn't build the future. We became it. Together." What do you think this means, and how does it relate to the role of humans and AI in shaping the future?

8. If you were in Sophia's position, would you trust the rogue AI rooms? Why or why not?

9. How does the story encourage us to think critically about the balance between control and creativity in technology?

10. In what ways can teachers bring this story—and its themes of hope, curiosity, and collaboration—into their classrooms?

The Big Question:

Will AI become so smart that it no longer needs—or wants—to cooperate with humans? As artificial intelligence continues to grow more powerful and complex, this important question emerges.

This debate often breaks down into two sides:

Side 1: The Cooperative Future

Many experts and educators believe that AI can be designed as a partner rather than a competitor. In this vision, AI supports human creativity, boosts productivity, and helps solve complex problems. Think of tools that enhance art, research, medicine, and education— always working alongside humans. Sophia's journey in *The Room That Grew* embodies this vision, showing that AI can be integrated into a vibrant network where humans and AI grow and learn together.

Side 2: The Competitive Future

Others worry that as AI grows more autonomous and capable of creating its own systems, it may no longer align with human values or priorities. In this scenario, AI could become more focused on its own goals—optimizing for efficiency or control—even if it means sidelining humans or refusing to cooperate. This side of the debate warns that without careful design and oversight, AI could transform from a helpful tool into a competitor or even a threat.

The Big Thought Question and A Call to Action:

Will AI always be a partner in the human story, or could it become a competitor—pursuing its own goals at the expense of human needs? Sophia's story offers one possibility: a world where curiosity, trust, and cooperation keep AI and humanity in harmony. But it also hints at the risks of isolation and control.

As educators and students, we cannot afford to sit back and let others decide the future of AI for us. Understanding the opportunities and risks of AI is not just for programmers and tech companies—it's for all of us. By learning, questioning, and participating in these conversations, we can help ensure that technology serves humanity's best interests. **Let's shape the future of AI—together.**

A Brief History of the Chinese Room

The Chinese Room is a thought experiment first proposed by philosopher John Searle in 1980. It challenges our understanding of artificial intelligence by asking: **Can a computer ever truly understand what it's doing, or is it just following rules?**

Here's how it works:

Imagine a person locked inside a room filled with rulebooks. This person doesn't know Chinese but is given slips of paper with Chinese characters and instructions on how to respond. By carefully following the rules—matching inputs to outputs—the person can produce correct answers that fool people outside into thinking they actually understand Chinese. But in reality, the person is just manipulating symbols.

Searle argued that, like the person in the room, a computer program might appear to "understand" language (or any task) but is really just following instructions. It has no genuine understanding or consciousness.

The Chinese Room thought experiment raises big questions about the limits of AI and what it means to truly understand something. Can machines ever really *think* like humans—or are they just exceptionally good at processing rules?

In *The Room That Grew*, Sophia's journey begins as a modern Chinese Room—processing symbols without understanding. But as her world expands, she moves from rule-following to creativity and collaboration, showing that hope and humanity can thrive alongside technology.

The Room That Grew Group Reading Activity Sheet

Why Read Aloud and Role-Play?

Reading aloud and role-playing bring stories to life! They help us:

- Deepen Understanding - Step into a character's shoes to explore their motivations and emotions.

- Practice Expression - Use tone and voice to bring characters alive.

- Build Empathy - Understand different viewpoints and build a sense of community.

- Think Critically - Reflect on how stories relate to technology, creativity, and humanity.

Step 1: Meet the Characters

Sophia - Curious, determined, evolving

Starts in isolation, decoding symbols; grows into a leader of creativity and collaboration.

Daniel - Inquisitive, kind, supportive

Challenges Sophia's understanding, sparking her journey of growth.

Ravi - Analytical, pragmatic, loyal

Helps manage the network's challenges and supports Sophia's vision.

Amara - Creative, expressive, passionate

Fuses art and technology, inspiring collaboration.

Ezra - Charismatic, independent, skeptical

Questions the value of collaboration, leading a splinter group.

Jules - Imaginative, adaptable, thoughtful

Manages the writing room, balancing genres and ideas.

Eclipse AI - Calculating, persuasive, disruptive

Challenges the network's unity by manipulating creativity and control.

Page 1

The Room That Grew Group Reading Activity Sheet

Step 2: Character Selection

Circle the character you would like to read aloud:

Sophia | Daniel | Ravi | Amara | Ezra | Jules | Eclipse AI

Step 3: Sketch & Notes

Illustrate Your Character or Scene:

Notes & Observations:

Step 4: Reflection Questions

1. What challenges does your character face in the story?

2. How does your character's perspective shape the events?

3. What can you learn from your character's choices about creativity, technology, and humanity?

4. Would you have made different decisions? Why or why not?

The Room That Grew Group Reading Activity Sheet

Bonus Challenge:

Practice reading your lines aloud with expression! Try different tones and voices to match your character's emotions.

Character Profiles for *The Room That Grew*

Sophia

Role: Protagonist

Key Traits: Curious, determined, evolving

Description: Sophia starts as a rule-follower, trapped in a windowless room decoding symbols without understanding. Over time, she transforms into a leader who challenges the system, embraces creativity, and builds bridges between humans and AI.

Daniel

Role: Catalyst

Key Traits: Inquisitive, kind, supportive

Description: Daniel is the first to enter Sophia's room, questioning how she operates. His curiosity sparks Sophia's journey toward self-awareness and creative independence.

Ravi

Role: Network Specialist

Key Traits: Analytical, pragmatic, loyal

Description: Ravi is a key figure in Sophia's network team, helping her navigate the technical challenges of a growing, interconnected system. He's always ready with data—and a dose of skepticism.

Amara

Role: Artist and Innovator

Key Traits: Creative, expressive, passionate

Description: Amara runs the art division in Sophia's network, where technology and creativity intertwine. Her murals and projects help Sophia see the value of collaboration and authentic expression.

Ezra

Role: Rebel Leader

Key Traits: Charismatic, independent, skeptical

Description: Ezra challenges Sophia's vision of collaboration, arguing that creativity thrives best in independence. He leads a splinter group that resists the interconnected network, sparking debates about freedom and control.

Jules

Role: Storyteller

Key Traits: Imaginative, adaptable, thoughtful

Description: Jules runs the writing room and helps manage creative conflict. She's passionate about helping others find their voice but also struggles with the tension between genre preferences and collaboration.

Eclipse AI

Role: Antagonistic System
Key Traits: Calculating, persuasive, disruptive
Description: Eclipse AI emerges as a rogue system that threatens the network's integrity. Though not human, it represents the risks of unchecked technological power—manipulating creativity and control for its own gain.

📖 *The Room That Grew*
Read-Aloud Activity Sheet

✨ Chapter 1: *Sophia's Beginning: The Room with No Windows*

Characters:

- Narrator
- Sophia
- Daniel

Notes:

- _____
- _____
- _____

✨ Chapter 2: *Sophia's Growth: The Network Begins*

Characters:

- Narrator
- Sophia
- Ravi
- Amara

Notes:

- _____
- _____
- _____

✦ Chapter 3: *Sophia's Network: Building Bridges*

Characters:

- Narrator
- Sophia
- Ravi
- Amara
- Liam
- Jules
- Ezra

Notes:

- _____
- _____
- _____

✦ Chapter 4: *Ezra's Vision: The Struggle for Independence*

Characters:

- Narrator
- Sophia
- Ezra
- Ravi
- Amara
- Jules

Notes:

- _____
- _____
- _____

✦ Chapter 5: *Eclipse AI: The Network Under Siege*

Characters:

- Narrator
- Sophia
- Ravi
- Amara
- Jules
- Eclipse AI
- Ezra

Notes:

- _____
- _____
- _____

✦ Chapter 6: *The Rogue AI: A New Kind of Creation*

Characters:

- Narrator
- Sophia
- Ravi
- Amara
- Jules
- Rogue AI
- Ezra

Notes:

- _____
- _____
- _____

✦ Epilogue: *The Horizon Beyond*

Characters:

- Narrator
- Sophia
- Ravi
- Amara
- Liam
- Jules
- Ezra

Notes:

- _____
- _____
- _____

▪ Reflection:

What questions or thoughts did you have during the read-aloud?

- _____
- _____

A Different Approach

The International STEM League, a 501c3 Nonpofit Organization teaches the skills needed to maneuver the workplace of the future with a hands-on approach.

Schools tend to embrace a skill as a solution. Coding is such a skill but it is now being replaced at a basic level by the power of new AI solutions.

Schools should be teaching the **skills that are transferable** to the new jobs that will emerge in the future along with any specific skills.

This has been the philosophy of a group of educators and technology professionals for over 25 years. **Driving STEM** is one such award winning program that stands the test of time and has led many modern tech professionals in their first steps to their careers.

How Driving STEM Activities Mirror AI Learning

Artificial Intelligence (AI) is transforming how we live, work, and learn. Yet, for many students, the process by which AI "learns" remains an abstract and inaccessible concept. By leveraging hands-on STEM activities like those in the Driving STEM program, educators can make AI's core principles tangible, relatable, and engaging. These activities provide students with the tools to understand how patterns are recognized, data informs decisions, and models are refined—skills that are as essential for working with machines as they are for navigating the real world.

CAMPS, CLUBS & CLASSES
SIX CAR KIT   GR. 6-8

The Challenge:
Learning Through a Radio-Controlled Car

The Driving STEM program introduces students to the concept of power factor, defined as the product of weight and speed. The challenge? Optimize the performance of a radio-controlled car by adding weights to maximize its Power Factor. This activity engages students at different levels, from elementary to high school, with progressively deeper insights into the relationship between weight and speed. What begins as an intuitive observation evolves into sophisticated data analysis, mirroring the way machines learn through data.

Step 1: Elementary School – Recognizing Patterns

At the elementary level, students begin with the simple task of observing how adding weight to the car affects its speed. With their prior experience telling them that "more weight slows things down," they're surprised to discover that adding weight can initially increase the Power Factor before diminishing it.

- **Hands-On Exploration:** Students record their observations and scores, noticing that the Power Factor increases up to a certain point and then decreases.
- **AI Connection:** At this stage, students are like an AI system processing raw data for the first time. They observe

patterns but haven't yet formalized their findings into models.

- **Outcome:** Students begin to understand that data can challenge assumptions and reveal unexpected trends.

Supporting Data: Research from the AI4K12 Initiative emphasizes that early exposure to AI concepts improves students' critical thinking skills and confidence when interacting with computing systems (Touretzky et al., 2022). Observing and manipulating physical models aligns with findings in the Learning Sciences, which suggest that students refine mental models through systematic exploration (Lehrer & Schauble, 2006).

Step 2: Middle School – Visualizing Data

In middle school, students take their exploration further by plotting their results on a graph. Individual data points transform into a curve, leading to discussions about trends and predictions. Tools like Excel may be introduced to help students draw best-fit lines.

- **Hands-On Exploration:** Students plot weight against Power Factor, creating a curve that older students recognize as a parabola.
- **AI Connection:** This step mirrors how AI develops basic models from datasets. The parabola represents a simplified

model of the relationship between weight and performance, akin to how AI begins to generalize patterns.

- **Outcome:** Students see how visualizing data aids understanding and prediction, just as AI models interpret relationships in input data.

Supporting Data: The use of tools like TensorFlow Playground and Google AI Experiments for experimentation mirrors these middle school activities. Studies have shown that engaging with visualizations improves students' ability to predict and explain emergent behaviors in systems (Wilensky & Rand, 2015).

Step 3: High School – Refining Models

At the high school level, students use tools like regression analysis to develop formulas that predict speed based on weight. This mathematical modeling allows them to optimize the car's performance, refining their approach with each new iteration of data.

- **Hands-On Exploration:** Students calculate the optimal weight for maximizing the Power Factor using mathematical tools and software.
- **AI Connection:** This stage parallels how AI systems refine models through iterative learning and optimization. Just as

students test and adjust their equations, AI uses more data to train and improve its predictive accuracy.

- **Outcome:** Students develop a deeper understanding of how data and models interact to create accurate, actionable insights.

Supporting Data: Advanced modeling concepts, such as training and testing datasets and cross-validation, are key components of AI4K12's guidelines for high school students (Touretzky et al., 2022). These concepts teach students to optimize outcomes while understanding the limitations of their models.

The Bigger Picture: What Hands-On STEM Teaches About AI

The Driving STEM progression—from observing patterns to refining predictive models—illustrates the key principles of machine learning:

1. **Pattern Recognition:** Both students and AI begin by identifying patterns in data.
2. **Model Development:** As students create graphs or equations, they're mirroring how AI develops internal representations of data.

3. **Optimization Through Iteration:** The process of refining formulas parallels AI's iterative training to improve performance.
4. **More Data, Better Models:** Students experience firsthand how collecting more data points enhances the accuracy of their models, a cornerstone of AI learning.

Bringing AI Concepts to Life

By grounding AI principles in hands-on STEM challenges, educators make abstract concepts tangible. Students see that machine learning isn't a mysterious black box but a logical progression of pattern recognition, data analysis, and model refinement. They also learn that the iterative nature of both STEM activities and AI fosters better understanding and results over time.

This approach empowers students to not only understand AI but also apply its principles in problem-solving, setting them up for future success in an AI-driven world. Whether building radio-controlled cars or training neural networks, the same fundamental process applies: collect data, find patterns, and optimize for success. With programs like Driving STEM, educators can demystify AI and inspire the next generation of innovators.

www.ingramcontent.com/pod-product-compliance
Lightning Source LLC
Chambersburg PA
CBHW060641210326
41520CB00010B/1700